BELGIUM

MAJOR WORLD NATIONS
BELGIUM

Noel Carrick

CHELSEA HOUSE PUBLISHERS
Philadelphia

Chelsea House Publishers

Contributing Author: Tom Purdom

Copyright © 1999, 2001 by Chelsea House Publishers,
a subsidiary of Haights Cross Communications.
All rights reserved.
Printed and bound in Malaysia.

5   7   9   8   6   4

Library of Congress Cataloging-in-Publication Data applied for

ISBN 0–7910–4735–0

CONTENTS

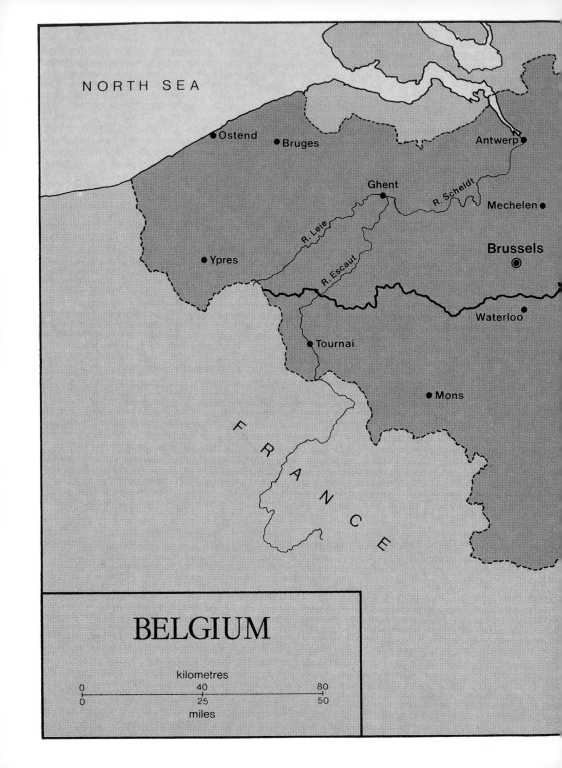

NORTH SEA

● Ostend

● Bruges

Antwerp ●

Ghent ●

R. Scheldt

Mechelen ●

R. Lele

Brussels
◉

● Ypres

R. Escaut

Waterloo ●

● Tournai

● Mons

F R A N C E

BELGIUM

kilometres

0   40   80
0   25   50

miles

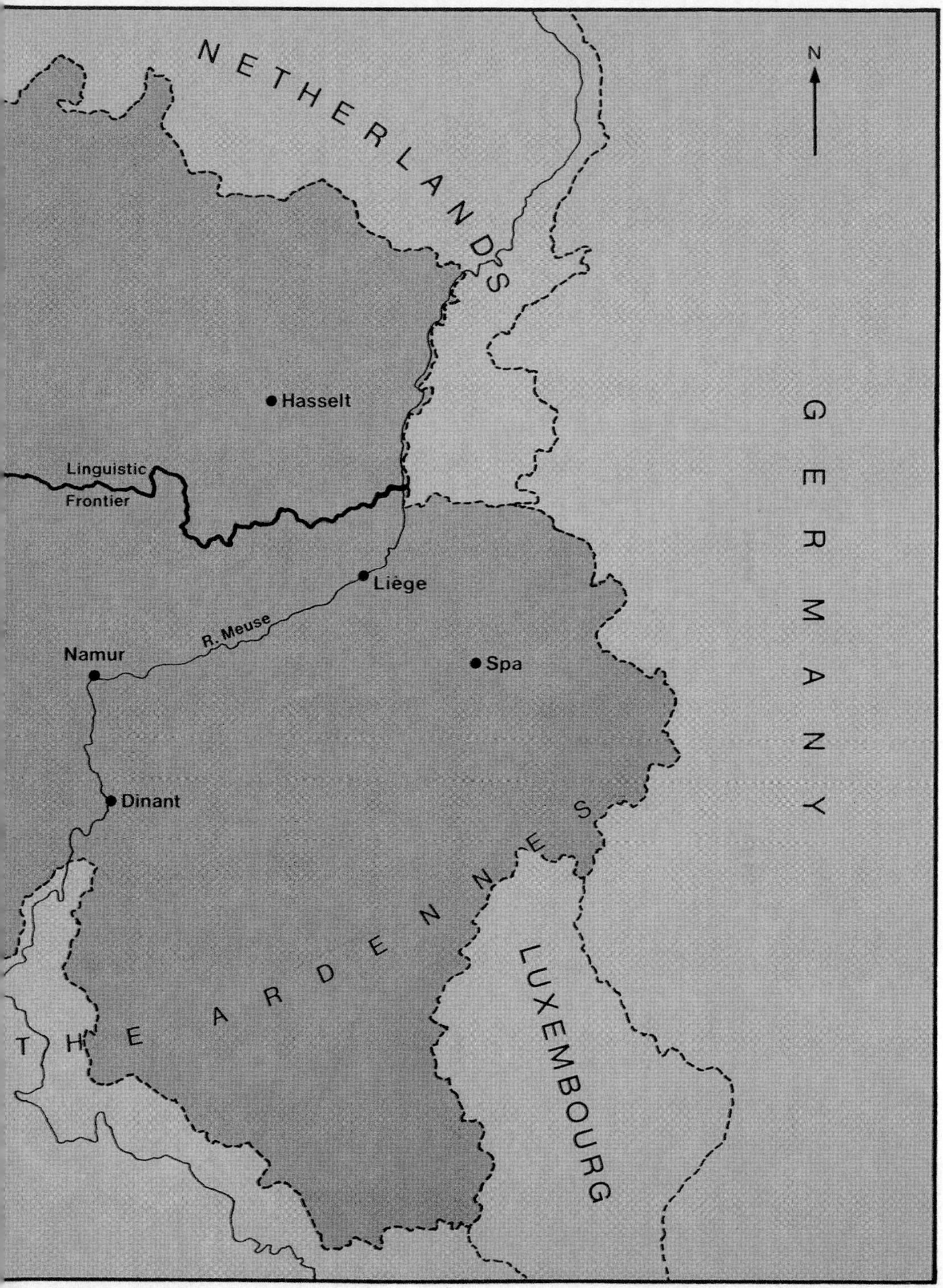

N
NETHERLANDS
GERMANY
Hasselt
Linguistic Frontier
Liège
R. Meuse
Namur
Spa
Dinant
THE ARDENNES
LUXEMBOURG

FACTS AT A GLANCE

Land and People

Official Name   Kingdom of Belgium

Location   Western Europe, bordering the North Sea between France and the Netherlands

Area   11,781 square miles (30, 513 square kilometers)

Climate   Moderate with cold winters and large amount of rainfall

Capital   Brussels

Other Cities   Antwerp, Liege, Ghent, Bruge

Population   10 million

Population Density   131 people per square mile (327 people per square kilometer)

Major Rivers   Meuse, Scheldt

Highest Point   Around Signal de Botrange (694 meters)

Official Language   Flemish (Dutch) in the north; French in the south; German in the east

Religions   Roman Catholic, 75 percent; Protestant, 25 percent

8

Literacy Rate	99 percent
Average Life Expectancy	77.35 years

Economy

Natural Resources	Coal, natural gas
Division of Labor Force	Agriculture, 2.6 percent; services, 69.7 percent; industry, 27.7 percent
Agricultural Products	Various fruits and vegetables
Other Products	Software, electronics
Industries	Petrochemicals, diamond, biochemistry
Major Imports	Fuels, grains, chemicals, foodstuff
Major Exports	Iron, steel, transportation equipment, diamonds, petroleum products
Major Trading Partners	European Union, United States
Currency	Belgian franc

Government

Form of Government	Federal parliamentary democracy under a constitutional monarchy
Government Bodies	Chamber of Deputies; Senate
Formal Head of State	King of the Belgians
Head of Government	Prime minister
Voting Rights	Compulsory for all citizens 18 years of age and older

HISTORY AT A GLANCE

150 B.C.	A Celtic tribe called the Belgae takeover the area now called Belgium.
51 B.C.	The Belgae fight the armies of Rome under Julius Caesar but are eventually defeated. The Belgae are led by their first national hero, Ambiorix. Roman rule of the area would last almost 400 years.
5th century A.D.	A Germanic tribe called the Franks settles in the area. When the Romans finally leave the lands, the Franks takeover and make it part of their empire. Christianity spreads throughout the area.
742 A.D.	Charlemagne is born in the Belgian city of Liège.
9th century	Charlemagne gains control over much of Europe and forms it into the Holy Roman Empire of which he becomes emperor. After his death his grandsons divide the empire between them, leading to great unrest and wars. Many Belgians are enslaved.
11th and 12th centuries	There is rapid growth in trade that brings economic prosperity to Europe. The city of Bruges becomes a busy trading center. The manufacture of cloth becomes Bruges' main industry.

15th century	A period of cultural enrichment occurs with the Dukes of Burgundy in control of the country. The textile industry is the mainstay of Belgium and much of northwestern Europe. Mary of Burgundy marries the emperor of the Austrian Empire, Maximilian, and the country comes under its influence.
16th century	The area that today makes up the Netherlands and Belgium comes under the influence of the Spanish king by marriage, and becomes known as the Spanish Netherlands. This is a time of great unrest in the area, much of it due to religious differences between Catholics and Protestants.
1608	The famous painter Peter Rubens becomes the court painter. The 17th century Flemish school of painters includes Rubens, Van Dyck, and Jordaens.
1701-1713	The Spanish War of Succession makes Belgium a battlefield. The war ends with the Treaty of Utrecht which makes Belgium part of the Austrian Empire.
1795	Belgium is invaded by the French army under Napoleon and it becomes part of his empire.
1815	The historic battle of Waterloo takes place on June 18th and Napoleon is defeated by Britain and her allies. Belgium is reunited with the Netherlands as one country.
1830	The Belgian revolution is fought and Belgium is declared an independent nation on October 4th.
1881-1885	King Leopold II seizes control of the Congo in Africa and Belgium becomes a colonial power.

The famous explorer Dr. Livingstone becomes part of the king's expeditionary force there.

1914-1918	In World War I, Belgium is invaded by Germany and many important battles are fought on Belgian soil.
1940-1944	Nazi Germany invades Belgium and the country is occupied through most of World War II. The Belgian government is exiled to London and King Leopold III is deported to Germany. The bloodiest battle of the war is fought on Belgian soil—the Battle of the Bulge.
late 1940's	Belgium experiences an economic resurgence following the war. Unrest occurs over the issue of the monarchy.
1949	Belgium joins the North Atlantic Treaty Organization (NATO).
late 1950s	Large-scale demonstrations occur over opposition to the colonial rule of the Belgian Congo.
1957	Belgium joins the European Economic Community and Brussels becomes its headquarters.
1960	In June Belgium grants independence to the Congo.
1970s and 1980s	Tensions between the ethnolinguistic groups of Belgium lead to major restructuring and constitutional reforms.
1977	Belgium is divided into three distinct regions—Flanders, Wallonia, and Brussels.
1992	The St. Michael's Agreement finalizes the division of Belgium into three regions, each with cul-

tural, economic, and educational autonomy. It lays the groundwork for the establishment of Belgium as a federal state.

1993 King Boudouin dies and is succeeded by his brother Albert.

1995 Belgium, along with seven other European Union countries, abolishes the need for passports and customs checks for any European Union citizens.

1996 Prime minister Jean-Luc Dehaene adopts economic austerity measures, raises taxes, and cuts social security benefits in an effort to improve the economy and to meet the economic requirements of the European Union single currency system.

1999 Coca-Cola institutes a massive recall of their products in Belgium after children at six different schools fall ill.

2000 Diesel rigs driven by members of the Belgian haulier's union cripple traffic in Brussels as protests over high fuel costs spread throughout Europe.

2001 Fears of foot-and-mouth disease spreading through Europe cease transport of livestock; suspicion of an infected pig in Belgium brings the ban to northern France; Eight people die in Belgium's worst train crash in 25 years when an empty train misses a red signal and collides with a packed commuter train.

1

Belgium—The Heart of Europe

Belgium is proof of the saying that good things come in small packages. It is one of the world's smallest countries, so small that Belgians often become international travelers when they go for a Sunday drive. They go to one, or more, of five countries during a brief outing–Belgium itself, France, Luxembourg, Germany, and the Netherlands.

The area of Belgium is only 11,781 square miles (30,513 square kilometers) but despite this there is great variety in the countryside. The terrain ranges from green rolling forested hills in the Ardennes region of the southeast, where there is skiing in winter, to flat plains and wide sandy beaches in the northwest where swimming is popular in summer. In some forests, the visitor can feel that he is in a remote and isolated corner of the world. But with 10 million inhabitants–131 persons to each square mile (327 per square kilometer)–Belgium is one of the most densely populated countries to be found anywhere on earth.

A typical view in the province of Luxembourg (not to be confused with Belgium's neighbor—the Grand Duchy of Luxembourg).

It lies at the "Crossroads of Europe," the geographical center of the most populous and heavily industrialized part of western Europe. And, throughout its history, it has been at the heart of Europe in a cultural, economic, and military sense as well.

Its land area is oddly shaped because, except for a 41-mile (67-kilometer) strip of coastline along the North Sea, it has no natural borders. Most nations have mountains, rivers, deserts, or long coastlines as barriers against neighboring countries. Belgium's illogical frontiers result from numerous treaties following wars, revolutions, and other political upheavals.

So much fighting has taken place over more than 2,000 years on Belgian soil that, with an area of northern France, it is known as the "Cockpit of Europe"—a cockpit was the name for a place where fierce fighting cocks often tore each other to pieces. Many of the battles did not directly concern the local people, but because Belgium either bordered on great powers like Britain, France, and Germany, or was ruled by others like Spain and Austria, it was the natural battleground. In particular, Belgium was the setting for many of the battles which periodically climaxed the hundreds of years of rivalry between Britain and France. Fighting occurred in Belgium as recently as World War I and World War II. Belgium is so identified with war that a Belgian flower, the Flanders Poppy—which grows profusely where the soil has been disturbed and is therefore abundant on churned-up battlefields—is recognized throughout the world as a symbol of soldiers killed in battle.

Although modern Belgium became a fully independent self-governing nation only in 1830, it is not correct to describe it as a relatively new country. Throughout its history, much of the area now known as Belgium was more or less regarded as a separate region, even though most parts were seldom independent of foreign rule.

Traveling along Belgium's splendid road system, one is seldom out of sight of a village, town, or city. This is partly because the northern part of the country is very flat, but it also reflects the sheer density of population. Nevertheless, the inhabitants enjoy a high standard of living because Belgium is a rich country. Many houses in Belgium are larger than those in other parts of Europe and the country is famous for its excellent food. Belgium is important on the international scene and the voice of its government is listened to with respect by leaders of other nations.

Belgium is a founder member of the European Economic

An aerial view of the Belgian countryside, showing the rich soil and the long narrow fields.

Community (EEC), now called the European Community (EC), which has its headquarters in Brussels. There are now 15 nations in the Community—and many citizens of these 15 countries live in Belgium to run the Community's affairs. So Belgium, and particularly, Brussels is very cosmopolitan. The employees of the EC are usually well-paid and their spending power makes a small contribution to Belgium's wealth.

Despite this outside influence, and the differences between Belgians themselves, Belgium is a compact and peaceful nation in

17

which the lifestyle is enriched not only by prosperity, pleasant countryside, and handsome cities, but also by an immensely rich cultural heritage.

It is a green country with high rainfall and the landscape is interlaced by wide rivers and canals, and dotted with lakes and ponds. The Meuse, the largest river, flows across the southern part of the country. In the past it was an important trade route and many towns and cities sprang up along its banks. The Scheldt River in the north is important because it links the port of Antwerp to the

Fishing in the Meuse River, Belgium's largest river.

sea. Belgium has some beautiful scenery—the landscape is rich and varied with rivers, wooded hills, valleys, green rolling pasturelands, and fields of growing crops.

The most notable beauty spots are in the Ardennes, and the Payottenland just east and south of Brussels. The Payottenland is sometimes called Brueghel-land because Pieter Brueghel, the Elder, included these landscapes in his paintings.

Nature has been generous but man has enriched the scene by building splendid cathedrals and churches, town halls and other public and private buildings. In the countryside, there are numerous castles and manor houses surrounded by tree-lined drives and woodlands. In the south, traditional stone farmhouses, built around a courtyard, provide a touch of the past.

Despite its small area, large population, and intense agricultural and industrial development, Belgium remains the habitat of wild animals, some in substantial numbers. Wild boar, hairy, fierce-looking and pig-like, several species of deer, and smaller fauna like otters, hedgehogs, badgers, and rabbits, live in the forests and fields. There are 60 species of wild animals and 300 species of birds.

Belgium sounds wonderful, and it is, but even the Belgians admit that their country has one drawback—its climate. Despite the moderating influence of the Gulf Stream, Belgium has cold winters and a high rainfall. Skies are often cloudy, even in summer, and many Belgians take summer holidays in the warmer climates of southern Europe. Despite the cold winter, it can become hot in summer, and the heat is often accompanied by high humidity.

However, the Belgians have evolved ways of living comfortably in their climate. Homes are solidly built, and are well-heated, as are buses, trains, and trolleys.

The wars that have marked Belgium's history, its geographical location, and the accident of history that made it the meeting place of two cultures, have combined to make this tiny country one of the most interesting spots on the globe.

A traditional farmhouse, built around a courtyard.

2

The Long Struggle for Independence

Belgium is named after a Celtic tribe called the Belgae—people who once occupied wide areas of Europe. The name Belgae comes from the Latin for "swollen" and historians think it originated from the baggy cloth trousers which the Belgae wore. They are believed to have moved into Belgium, from what is now Germany, about 150 years before the birth of Christ. It is not known whether they fought and drove out the people who were already there but this seems likely.

The next major event in Belgian history was the arrival of Julius Caesar. Caesar's task was to capture Gaul for the Roman Empire. At that time Gaul included present-day France, Switzerland, Luxembourg, and even parts of northern Italy.

One by one the Gallic tribes were defeated by Caesar's legions but the Belgae resisted for seven years. They were tough, ruthless fighters who objected to the Romans intruding onto their territory although they themselves had not been there long. At one time it looked as if they might manage to halt the Romans but finally, in 51 B.C., the Belgae were defeated. Belgium's first national hero was Ambiorix who led the Belgae in their struggle against the Romans.

Once conquered, the Belgae quickly adopted Roman ways and began to speak Latin. Latin was not the only language in use because other tribes called Franks were allowed to settle in the area, mainly in the fifth century A.D., and they spoke a Germanic language. During Roman rule, which lasted about 400 years, the area became important for farming and trading. Many cities and towns which still exist today were founded during this period.

When the Romans finally left, the Franks established an empire with its capital at Tournai. Clovis, who later became king of the Franks and the most powerful man in northern Europe, was born at Tournai in 465 A.D. He brought together tribes from all over Gaul, founded an empire, and made Paris its capital. Although "Belgian" by birth, Clovis is regarded as a hero by the French because he was the founder of France.

After the time of Clovis, the history of Belgium becomes very complicated. It was not until another great king of the Franks, Charlemagne, emerged to found the greatest European empire since Roman times, that it is possible to pick up the threads again.

Charlemagne, also known as Charles the Great, was born near the Belgian city of Liège in 742 or 743 A.D. Through his skill as a soldier and his ability to convince people that he could give them peace and prosperity, he extended his power over a vast region which he called the Holy Roman Empire. It covered much of the European part of the first Roman Empire, and it was "Holy" because Charlemagne was a Christian and wanted those he ruled to be Christians. His capital was at Aachen, a city now in Germany but only a short distance from the Belgian border. Aachen was once known by its French name Aix-La-Chapelle. After Charlemagne's death, his grandsons squabbled over who would become emperor and finally divided the empire between them.

Fragments of the empire were subsequently claimed by various kings and princes of parts of Germany and France, and Belgium became, over a 300-year period, a series of small principalities, many of them under the control of these outsiders. Wars and revolts were frequent. One area which remained independent was the Principality of Liège which was ruled by a Prince-Bishop. It was one of the few parts of Belgium to escape foreign domination.

These were unhappy times. There were incessant wars and many Belgians were forced to become serfs. They lived like slaves, were not permitted to leave the place where they were born and were frequently forced to serve in the armies of their masters. In addition, Belgium, like many parts of Europe in this era, was constantly raided by Vikings from Scandinavia who burned villages, stole stock and other property, and often killed without mercy.

Although the serfs were unaware of it, things were happening that would eventually make their lives better. During this period European kings and noblemen, including many from Belgium, went on Crusades to the Middle East. They wanted to free the places where Christ had lived from the Saracens (Muslim warriors who had conquered much of the Middle East). One Belgian Crusader, Godfrey de Bouillon actually ruled Jerusalem for a time

Liège, on the Meuse River. This city is now a mixture of very old and very new buildings.

after it had been captured from the Saracens.

Although it had not been their aim to do so, the Crusaders opened up trade routes to the East which had been closed since the fall of the first Roman Empire. Many parts of Belgium became prosperous by making goods to sell in these newly-opened markets. Cities like Ghent and Bruges in Flanders became large and rich from the manufacture of cloth and other items, and Belgium

24

emerged as one of the most important economic regions of Europe. This prosperity filtered down to the lower levels and both the serfs on the land and particularly the skilled craftsmen in the cities became more free, even powerful, with some groups forming their own armies.

In 1384 an event occurred that seemed unimportant at the time, but which was to change Belgium and ensure that the country was dominated by foreigners for the next 450 years. The event was the marriage between the beautiful daughter of the ruler of Flanders (a Belgian principality) and a man called Philip the Bold, from Burgundy. As a result of his marriage, Philip became ruler of Flanders and he and his descendants gradually increased the size

A peaceful scene in the old city of Bruges.

of their Belgian territory. Nearly 100 years later a descendant called Mary of Burgundy married Maximilian, the Emperor of Austria (a descendant of Charlemagne) and much of Belgium became associated with the Austrian Empire.

The son of Maximilian and Mary, Philip the Handsome, married a Spanish princess and Spain became involved in Belgium's affairs. Their son who was born in Ghent in 1500 became both King Charles I of Spain and Emperor Charles V of Germany. Charles spent much of his time in Ghent, which was then far larger than Paris. Other Belgian cities such as Antwerp were also important at this time, and Brussels, which later became the capital, had also begun to increase in importance. The area which is today the Netherlands and Belgium was then called the Spanish Netherlands.

In 1555, Charles V handed the throne of the Spanish Netherlands to his son Philip, who became Philip II of Spain in the following year.

From 1559 there were constant uprisings throughout the kingdom. Religious differences were an important cause of the unrest—the northern part of the Spanish Netherlands was largely Protestant while the southern provinces were Catholic. The history of this period is very complicated but Philip's troops managed to recapture the whole of the southern part of the Netherlands—the area which is now Belgium. The northern provinces became an independent Protestant state, now called the Kingdom of the Netherlands or Holland. Many people who disliked Spanish rule left Belgium and went to Holland—Belgium suffered as a result of

Old buildings in the city of Ghent, originally a center for the manufacture of cloth.

this migration of skills and money. One lasting effect of these events is that Belgium is still mainly Catholic, while Holland is mainly Protestant.

The next century saw some of the most intense fighting and strife Belgium has known. France invaded in an attempt to wrest Belgium from the Spaniards and Britain became involved. The Treaty of Utrecht in 1713 made Belgium a part of the Austrian Empire but, following the French Revolution, the French invaded twice and took Belgium from the Austrians. Napoleon visited this newly-acquired part of his empire in 1803. Napoleon was finally defeated at the Battle of Waterloo, south of Brussels by Britain and her allies under the command of the Duke of Wellington. This historic battle took place on June 18, 1815—50,000 men were killed. After Napoleon's fall, a conference of European powers re-united Belgium with the kingdom of the Netherlands but this arrangement did not last long.

When Belgium was rejoined to the Netherlands, the Dutch ruler, William I, tried to please his new citizens in the south. But he made mistakes, one of which was to try to make Dutch the official language of Brussels and some other places. It was a performance of an opera which sparked off the Belgian Revolution that finally brought independence. In 1830, "The Mute Woman of Portici" was staged at the Théâtre Royal de la Monnaie, the famous Brussels opera house. The opera is about the people of the Italian city of Naples and their attempts to throw out the Spaniards who ruled them in the 17th century. The people of Brussels interpreted the opera as a message that they should try to free themselves from the Dutch. Fighting broke out in the streets, a provisional government was formed and this proclaimed Belgium an independent nation on October 4, 1830. It has remained independent ever since.

For a short time Belgium was, like many other European nations, a colonial power. The story of how King Leopold II acquired his colony in Central Africa is long and complicated. However, in 1885, he became sovereign of the Congo Free State, a role quite separate from his position as king of the Belgians.

Many people criticized the activities of the king's officials in the Congo, but some improvements were made during his reign. He put an end to the activities of Arab slave traders who periodically

The Théâtre Royal de la Monnaie, the Brussels opera house. It was a performance here which planted the seeds of the revolution which was to lead to Belgium's independence in 1830.

raided villages, to carry off the inhabitants and sell them as slaves. King Leopold also organized the exploration and mapping of most of the territory. One of the men engaged in this task was Henry Morten Stanley who later found Dr. Livingstone deep in the African jungle and introduced himself with the now famous remark "Dr. Livingstone, I presume."

The Belgians were, for various reasons, reluctant to become a colonial power. But, in 1908, the Belgian nation took control of the Congo from the king. Thousands of Belgians poured into the area. Many went to exploit its mineral riches, such as copper, but others went to help the indigenous people.

Like many colonial powers, Belgium found that the first people to oppose her rule were those she had trained and educated. In the 1950s Belgium realized that attitudes and conditions had changed and her presence was no longer welcomed by many local people. She therefore decided to relinquish control and, in 1960, the Congo became the independent state of Zaire. Many Belgians remained in Zaire after independence, but the loss of the colony was a severe blow to the Belgian economy.

Many of the important battles of World War I were fought on Belgian soil. There were major engagements at Mons in 1914 and at Ypres in 1914, 1915, and 1917. Hundreds of thousands died in the fighting. War cemeteries with their somber ranks of cement headstones and crosses are scattered across the landscape of West Flanders—stark reminders of the French, Belgian, American, British, and other Allies who died.

Belgians are proud that they managed to retain control of a small part of their country during World War I. But in World War II they were not so fortunate and Belgium was occupied by German forces for most of the war. Her people suffered great hardships and many of them, including Jews, were incarcerated or executed in Breendonck, a fortress between Brussels and Antwerp. This fortress has been preserved as a national monument to the memory of Belgium's struggles during the occupation.

One of the bitterest and bloodiest engagements of the war, the Battle of the Bulge (so-called because of the configuration of the battlefront), was fought on Belgian soil between the Germans and the Americans. The Germans who were being forced back towards Germany by the Allies counterattacked in Wallonia near the city of Bastogne.

Belgium has now seen no fighting for over 50 years. This is one of the longest periods of continuous peace in its history and one which the Belgians hope is permanent.

The American cemetery in the province of Liège—a reminder of the fact that many foreign soldiers killed in the First and Second World Wars are buried in Belgium.

3

The Institutions of Government

Belgium is a free, democratic, and very liberal nation. However, because of its history and its linguistic problems, it is not an easy country to govern.

Belgian politicians embrace a wide spectrum of political ideas, from right to left. This means that there are many political parties—at least eight major parties and several minor ones. The voting system, which is called proportional representation, ensures that many of these parties have members in parliament. As a result, all Belgian governments are coalitions. In a coalition government several parties combine temporarily to form a government even though their policies may differ on a number of issues. A disadvantage of this system is that, should one party in the coalition decide to withdraw, the government may fall. If this happens the politicians will attempt to form another coalition, but if that fails it may be necessary to call a general election. The difficulties of coalition government are not unique to Belgium. They are com-

The Belgian parliament building in Brussels.

mon to most countries with proportional representation, Italy being another example.

Belgium's parliament, like those in the United States and Britain, has two houses. This means that there are two separate groups of people who meet to frame laws and decide what actions the government will take. The Chamber of Deputies has 150 member called deputies, and the Senate has 71 members called senators. All the members of the Chamber of Deputies are elected, but only two-thirds of the senators are elected. The other senators are chosen by provincial councils, by the Senate itself, or they have an automatic right to a seat because of their position.

Elections must be held at least every four years. However, parliaments do not always last that long because governments sometimes call elections early if they think they have a good chance of being re-elected.

The two Houses of Parliament have equal power. Bills can be introduced in either House but do not become law until they have been passed by both Houses and signed by the king.

The Belgian parliament is multilingual. Members of parliament address the House in their own language (which may be French or Dutch). Their speeches are translated by interpreters, despite the fact that most deputies and senators probably speak both major languages. All members of parliament belong to the Cultural Council of their linguistic community. These Cultural Councils oversee cultural activities in their part of the country.

Belgium is divided into ten provinces and 596 local municipalities, called communes. The ten provinces are Antwerp, Flemish Brabant, Walloon Brabant, Hainaut, West Flanders, East Flanders, Liège, Limburg, Namur and Belgian Luxembourg. (The Belgian province of Luxembourg should not be confused with the Grand Duchy of Luxembourg which is an independent country on Belgium's southeastern border). The citizens of these ten provinces elect provincial councils and the king appoints provincial governors.

Until 1977 there were 2,359 communes but many of these have

merged and there are now 696. Communes have a council comprising a mayor, called a burgomaster, councillors, and aldermen. Councils are elected every six years. Communes do not have the same language complications as the national parliament because the citizens of each commune speak the same language. There are some exceptions in the Brussels area. Officially, the king appoints burgomasters but the person concerned is always nominated by the commune.

Belgium is undergoing a process called "regionalization" which means that some powers are being transferred from the central government to the regions of Wallonia and Flanders. For instance, there are Ministries of Culture for each region, and these control most aspects of education. However, matters like defense and foreign affairs, which are concerned with Belgium's relations with other countries, are still under the control of central government.

Despite these inherent divisions, Belgium is a calm, peaceful nation apart from occasional political and industrial demonstrations. Most Belgians are law-abiding citizens and enjoy living in a country where law and order is respected.

Belgium is a constitutional monarchy. The head of state is called the King of the Belgians. The king reigns but does not govern; he appoints and dismisses ministers, but only in consultation with his government. He may also call or dismiss parliament. No action is effective unless countersigned by a minister of the government. The king's powers and duties closely resemble those of the British monarch. He is also commander-in-chief of the armed forces.

Prince Leopold of Saxe-Coburg was elected the first "King of the

Belgians" by the Belgian National Congress on June 4, 1831, a few months after Belgium became independent. He became King Leopold I on July 21st that year and July 21st is still Belgium's National Day.

Leopold was 40 when he became king. He was a dashing figure who excelled at military tactics, had reached the rank of general in the Russian army, and had fought in the campaigns against Napoleon.

He was also an intellectual and had learned Latin and Greek while very young. He married an English woman, Princess Charlotte of Wales who died in 1817, and was very much influenced by her. Queen Victoria was his niece.

An equestrian portrait of Leopold I, the first king of the Belgians.

Former King Baudouin I, and his wife Queen Fabiola.

Leopold I died in 1865. He was succeeded by his second son, Leopold II who made Belgium a colonial power by acquiring the Belgian Congo. The territory was rich in minerals and was a source of enormous wealth for Belgium.

Leopold II's successors were Albert I, Leopold III, Baudouin I, and the present king, Albert II. The Belgian throne can only be passed on through the male line, so if the king has no son, the crown passes to the oldest son of the king's oldest brother.

Like the British monarch, the king of the Belgians is traditionally non-political; in this way he avoids antagonizing any of his subjects.

4

Language—a Delicate Question

Visitors to Belgium quickly realize that there is something unusual about the place names. Anyone traveling south along the major highway from the Dutch border, comes to a signpost marked *Bergen*. A few miles on, the signpost says *Bergen-Mons*, and further on, it says simply *Mons*. All three signs are for the same city which is known in English by its French name, Mons.

Mons is in the south. The people who live there call it Mons; people in the north call it Bergen; and those in Brussels use its name in both languages. Many cities have two, even three, names. Liège, for example, has three names: *Liège* in French; *Luik* in Dutch and, as it is close to the German border, *Lüttich* in German.

This confusion with road signs highlights the language problems in Belgium. Belgium's population falls into two distinct language groups, and to complicate matters, there is a very small third language group.

An invisible line called the Linguistic Frontier runs from east to west, dividing the country almost exactly in half. The area to the north is called Flanders, the people are called Flemings, and their official language is Dutch. To the south, the area is called Wallonia, the people are called Walloons and their official language is French. The third area is in the east of the country with its center at Eupen. Here the people speak German, but they are a small minority of only 65,000. Thus Belgium has three official languages: Dutch, French, and German.

Newspapers, literature, government publications and education are in Dutch for the Flemings and in French for the Walloons. However, many people do not use the official language in their everyday lives. In Flanders, many people speak Flemish and in Wallonia they speak Walloon. Neither Flemish nor Walloon is a single language. Flemish is a number of dialects or accents based on Dutch, and Walloon comprises dialects or accents based on French. When Flemings talk to people from other parts of Flanders, they speak Dutch. But when they speak to somebody from their own area or city, they speak the local variety of Flemish. The same applies in Wallonia where people converse with neighbors in Walloon but in French with people further away in Wallonia.

In general, Western Europe is divided into peoples of Germanic culture and languages and those of Romance culture and languages. Most Romance languages, including French, Italian and Spanish are heavily influenced by Latin, the language of the ancient Romans. This was spread throughout Europe, and

These signs with their Dutch and French names are just one indication of the fact that Belgium has more than one official language.

beyond, more than 2,000 years ago. In Belgium these two languages and cultures meet.

Why is the Linguistic Frontier in Belgium and not further north or south? This question is hard to answer because historians cannot agree among themselves. A likely reason is that when the Romans ruled Belgium they allowed people whom they called "barbarians" to enter their territory and settle. They were not really barbarians but the Romans called everybody who was not a Roman "a barbarian." These particular "barbarians" were known as Franks and they spoke a Germanic language. The Roman army had a line of forts across Belgium and the Franks stopped somewhere near this line. So although the original inhabitants and the

40

Franks mixed, those living to the north of the line of forts continued to speak the Germanic language—which over hundreds of years developed into modern German, English, and Dutch. Those living to the south of the forts spoke Latin, which developed into the Romance languages.

Many people believe that the Linguistic Frontier shifted many times after the Romans left northern Europe and may have continued to do so for about 600 years. We know its position had become firmly fixed by about the 13th century A.D.

There are many Belgians who cannot converse with each other because they cannot speak the same language, and instead of more Belgians learning the language of the other part of the country, fewer are doing so. Many young people in Flanders speak much

A fish stall in Ostend. The shellfish are labelled in both Dutch and French.

better English than French. This is because English, being a Germanic language, is easier for them to learn. They also believe English will be more valuable if they make their careers in business. However, many people in Flanders speak French and many people in Wallonia speak Dutch. Nevertheless, this difference in languages does cause problems.

In Brussels and its environs most people are truly bilingual, that is to say they speak both languages. Officially, Brussels uses both languages and each is in common use. This raises an interesting question. When two residents of Brussels who do not know each other meet—for instance when a woman speaks to a shop assistant—in which language would she start the conversation? Brussels residents say they tend to begin a conversation with a stranger in their mother tongue. Although people in Brussels are bilingual, one of the two languages is their mother tongue. This is literally the language in which their mother spoke to them when they first began to talk. Conductors checking tickets on Brussels' suburban trains are careful to ask for tickets in both languages, and officials employed in public places such as post offices are also careful to use both languages.

Unfortunately, a Belgian's name will not always indicate his or her mother tongue, for many people whose mother tongue is French have Flemish-sounding names and vice versa. Some names combine French and Flemish—Jean Luc Vanassche, or Karel Dupont, for example. In Brussels the language differences are more obvious than in other cities because everything is in both languages. All over Brussels there are pairs of signposts, advertising boarding, public transportation notices, even street names, one in French and one in Dutch. This is confusing for the visitor who finds that a street called the *Avenue des Arts* in French, becomes *Kunstlaan* in Dutch.

The language difference is reflected in the media. There are four state-owned television channels, two broadcasting in Dutch and two in French. Sometimes a Dutch language channel will show a French language program or vice versa, but there are always subtitles in the other language. The main French and Dutch radio stations are also run by the government, but there are a growing number of small privately-owned local stations. There is no advertising on Belgian state television or radio. Viewers in Belgium can see more television channels than anywhere else in Europe. Most Belgians subscribe to cable television which gives access to up to 32 stations.

In Brussels, the major daily newspapers and periodicals are either in French or Dutch and those in provincial cities are in the language of the area. Despite the language barrier, the Brussels press is lively and highly professional and its coverage of local and international news is excellent.

A further example of the difference between the two parts of Belgium is their national days—which are celebrated on different dates. The Belgian National Day is July 21, the anniversary of the day in 1831 when Leopold I became the first king of the Belgians. Flanders and Wallonia celebrate their own regional national days with as much energy as they celebrate the Belgian National Day and each has it own emblems and flag. The emblem of Wallonia is

The Belgian flag—one of the necessities for an independent country is to have its own distinctive flag. Belgium became independent in 1830.

a splendidly colored rooster and that of Flanders is the Flemish lion. The Belgian national flag, a simple design of thick black, yellow, and red vertical stripes, is flown on appropriate occasions all over the country.

5

A Religion in Common

One thing that many Belgians have in common is their religion: a large percentage are Catholics. Nobody knows the exact figures because the government believes in complete religious freedom and does not collect figures on its citizens' religious beliefs. However, it is generally assumed that more than nine out of ten Belgians think of themselves as Catholics.

Religious events play an important part in Belgian family life. Babies are baptized soon after birth and children make their First Communion when they are six or seven. The First Communion Day is a cause for celebration. Traditionally the girls dress in white and the boys wear their finest clothes. Friends and relatives go to the church service and attend a family gathering afterwards. A few years later, children publicly participate in a second Holy Communion service which is often combined with Confirmation. This is also an occasion for a family gathering.

Under Belgian law, couples getting married must participate in a civil ceremony. However, most couples also have a church wed-

ding which, like all Belgian family events, is followed by a sump-
tuous feast.

The Catholic Church has exerted an important influence
throughout Belgian history. That influence has declined in recent
years but the Church or Catholic organizations are still involved
in Belgian life in ways that do not openly occur even in other
Catholic countries. There are, for example, Catholic trade unions
and political parties. There are a large number of church build-

**The cathedral at Tournai, the one-time capital of the Empire of the
Franks.**

ings— magnificent cathedrals, parish churches, schools and hundreds of religious shrines dotted along roads and country lanes.

The Church in Belgium has produced many great men, from high-ranking cardinals down to humble rural priests. One of the greatest, known all over the world, was Father Damien de Veuster who, in 1873, went to care for lepers on the island of Molokai in the Pacific. He died of leprosy after years of selflessly caring for those unfortunate people. His love and care for the lepers, knowing that sooner or later he must catch their disease and die from it, is one of the great modern individual acts of personal bravery. Father Damien came from the small Flemish village of Tremelo, and the farm where he was born and raised is now a museum depicting his life. He is buried in a church in Leuven and many people make a pilgrimage to this shrine.

Belgians are very tolerant about religion and the small minorities of Protestants, Jews, and Muslims can practice their religions openly. Many Jewish people live in Antwerp where some are active in the diamond business. There is also a large Jewish community in Brussels. Most of the Muslims in Belgium have moved there comparatively recently from North Africa. They live mainly in the inner suburbs of Brussels.

6

Agriculture

Belgians love to eat well, but where does the excellent food come from? Belgian farmers produce more than 70 percent of the agricultural produce consumed in Belgium. This is a remarkable feat, because only one-fourth of the total land area is available to agriculture, and there is a large population to be fed. About three percent of Belgians work in agriculture and their produce contributes nearly three percent to the gross national product.

Some Belgian farms are small, many between 22 and 52 acres (between one hectare and 21 hectares). Some are inefficient but others are very specialized and use intensive cultivation methods, resulting in high production from small areas. Larger farms tend to be efficient as they can afford to invest in the most modern machinery. They have larger fields and can therefore use larger and faster equipment.

The major crops in Belgium are barley, which is important for the beer industry, oats, wheat, maize, fodder such as clover for cattle, and sugar beet. Tobacco, flax and hops are also grown.

Flax, drying in the fields in West Flanders. It is the raw material for the production of the linen thread used in lace-making.

Beet has been grown in Belgium since the early 19th century when an efficient process was developed for large-scale extraction of sugar from beet. (This process evolved as a result of an Allied blockade of Europe—at the time dominated by Napoleon—which prevented the import of cane sugar. Ironically, one of Europe's largest beet sugar extracting plants was built in the mid-19th century at Waterloo, where Napoleon was defeated. It is still standing but is no longer used).

Cattle farming is important—cattle are raised for the beef trade and there are also large herds of dairy cows. There are pig farms all over Belgium, and many regions have special ways of preparing

49

hams and other pork products. These prepared pork meats are known collectively as *charcuterie*.

With a large population to feed, market gardening is obviously a major business and there are extensive areas under glass. Grapes are grown in heated glasshouses, mainly near Overijse on the outskirts of Brussels. These vines are not grown for wine, but produce a large juicy fruit for eating. They are a great delicacy and quite expensive. The Belgian climate is not suitable for growing wine grapes outdoors, so Belgium imports most of its wine.

Belgium is a major exporter of fruit and fresh vegetables. Endive is flown in large quantities to North America during the season and Belgian asparagus is famous.

Flowers and plants are also important, with the country exporting more than 50,000 tons each year, mainly to neighboring coun-

Heated glasshouses in Brabant where grapes are grown. Belgium's dessert grapes are famous—and delicious!

Children at a fish stall in Ostend. Most of the fish eaten in Belgium is caught by Belgian fishermen.

tries. The most popular flowers are roses, azaleas, begonias, and orchids which are all grown under glass.

Production of chickens for the table, and of eggs, is a huge industry, mostly carried out on a large scale in "factories." It is estimated that at any given time there are more than 30,000,000 hens and chickens in Belgium.

Most of the fish eaten in Belgium is caught by Belgian fishermen, but mussels are imported from the Netherlands. In fact, almost all the Dutch mussel harvest finds its way across the border into Belgium.

Belgium carries out almost all of its own food processing. The country is a food exporter, mainly of high quality gourmet items such as beer, sugar, vegetable oils and canned food.

51

A farming village in West Flanders.

Agricultural production in Belgium is divided into a number of zones, some overlapping. For example, the region to the south and northwest is mainly pastoral with many areas of the Ardennes producing beef cattle. The soil in this region is not suitable for other types of farming. The flat plains of West Flanders are mainly used for mixed farming; and a strip across the center of the country, where the soil is suitable, produces most of the wheat and sugar beet.

Belgian farmers, like all farmers in the European Community, receive guaranteed prices for many of their products under a scheme known as the Common Agricultural Policy.

7

Industry and Commerce

Belgium has been an important trading nation for centuries—importing raw materials and exporting manufactured goods. The country industrialized early in the 19th century, very soon after Britain's industrial revolution. Because of this combination of industry and trade Belgium, though small, is a rich country. But, like every other industrialized nation, Belgium today faces economic problems and many of its old industries, particularly steelmaking, are now in decline.

The Walloon iron and steel industry developed because there were large deposits of coal at Mons, La Louvière, Charleroi, and Liège. Most of Wallonia's remaining coal deposits are in thin seams, deep underground which makes extraction difficult and therefore expensive. Also, a lot of the equipment is now out-of-date and inefficient. For all these reasons production costs are higher than in some other countries and it is now cheaper to import coal. A program to rationalize and modernize the coal industry has been under way for several years. Wallonia and Flanders still produce significant tonnages and extraction has expanded recently in the Flemish region of Campine near the city of Hasselt.

A century and a half of coal and steel production have left their mark on the Walloon landscape. Huge mounds of spoil from the coal mines and the skeletons of abandoned steel works are scattered across the landscape—reminders of the region's prosperous past.

Besides making major contributions to the country itself,

The landscape of Wallonia bears witness to the industrial nature of the area: these mounds of spoil are the outward signs of the coal and steel industry.

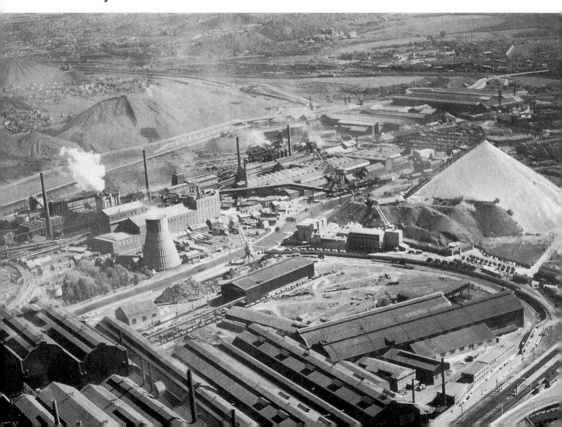

Belgian coal and steel production has helped develop the technology of the world's mining and metal industries. Processes developed in Wallonia in the heyday of the steel industry are still in use in steel plants worldwide. Belgium has also contributed to the technology of other metal industries. For example, a Belgian chemist, Daniel Dony from Liège, developed a process for production of the non-ferrous metal zinc early in the 19th century. Factories in Belgium near the German border remain among the world's top zinc refiners. Belgium once had deposits of zinc but these have long been exhausted and unrefined zinc must now be imported.

Engineering firms, using steel, were set up soon after the Belgian steel industry was established. Belgium developed an expertise in mechanical engineering which it has maintained. Belgian engineering firms, many of them more than 100 years old, still develop and produce new products. Even before the Industrial Revolution, the Liège area was famous for the manufacture of weapons—today guns and other arms are still produced there. Belgium once produced an automobile, called the Minerva, which rivaled the Rolls Royce in the quality of its engineering. The Minerva is no longer produced but it is now a collector's item and fetches a high price.

The products of Belgium's modern manufacturing industries range from plastics to clothing, and from chemicals to glass. Belgium also has some traditional industries, many of them centuries old. These older industries depend on the skill of the workforce. The diamond cutting industry in Antwerp, for example, employs hundreds of skilled technicians who painstakingly cut rough diamonds into glittering centerpieces for fine jewelry. A diamond is expensive and one false cut can destroy it or reduce its value considerably. Merchants from Antwerp are also active in world diamond trading; this involves exchange of stones on trust, so buyers and sellers must have complete confidence in each other's honesty. Belgium is also a major producer of diamond cutting equipment.

Another even more traditional Belgian industry is lacemaking. Lace is made from linen which comes from the flax plant grown in Flanders. Some say the craft originated in Belgium but this claim is disputed. However, lace has been made there for many centuries and Belgian handmade lace is of exquisite beauty. Since the Middle Ages, well-dressed women have used it to edge their finest clothing and to decorate their homes. Although Flanders is the most important lacemaking region, beautiful lace is also made at Binche in Wallonia and in Brussels where very fine thread is used.

Lacemaking by hand requires nimble fingers and patience. One kind of lace, known abroad as Malines, was so intricate that it took a highly skilled lacemaker 14 days to produce a yard (one meter). Women can still sometimes be seen making lace, their fingers dexterously maneuvering small bobbins.

Belgium has long been a producer of many different kinds of fabric. Carpets have been made there for centuries and the wealth of Ghent and Bruges was based on cloth weaving.

Perhaps the most traditional Belgian industry is brewing beer. Belgians are among the world's major consumers of beer—simply because their beer is excellent. Beer is made by brewing malt,

Brewing vats in the Piedboeuf Brewery in Liège. Belgian beer is excellent.

which is derived from barley, with various other ingredients. The ancient Egyptians are believed to have made a kind of beer thousands of years ago. We know that the Celts in Belgium, and Germanic tribes from nearby, were brewing a beer-like drink from barley when the Romans invaded over 2,000 years ago.

Beer drinkers in Brussels have an old saying "While there is Geuze, there is Brussels." Geuze is one of about 400 different varieties of beer brewed in Belgium. It is unique because, unlike other beers, the brewer does not add yeast to make the liquid ferment. Fermentation is caused by a yeast which occurs naturally, floating in the air. Geuze takes two years to brew and can only be produced in a very small area of the Payottenland, near Brussels, because the yeast is not present in the air elsewhere.

Present-day Belgians do not drink as much beer as their grandfathers. At the turn of the century there were 3,200 breweries and

57

Belgians drank an average of 44 gallons (200 liters) of beer per year. Today they drink about 7 gallons (32 liters) per head per year and there are only about 300 breweries. It is the variety, not the volume, which makes the Belgian beer industry so different from that of any other country.

Monks have made beer in their monasteries since the Dark Ages. Five monasteries and several commercial breweries make a strong, richly-flavored beer called *Trappiste* which is named after a monastic order.

There are many other beers which are unique to Belgium—White Beer, for example, a cloudy drink flavored with coriander and orange peel. A company once produced a large wall poster showing the labels of most beers brewed in Belgium—people gave up counting the labels after they reached 300. Belgians are so fond of sampling different varieties of beer that some breweries in Britain produce special beers just for export to Belgium.

Finally, another special Belgian industry is the manufacture of delicious chocolates. Freshly made, these chocolates are tangy and mouth-watering and are popular throughout the world. However, the Belgians themselves adore their own chocolates so much that they eat most of the nation's production before it can be exported.

8

Education

The education system, like so many aspects of Belgian life, is divided along linguistic lines. Children in Flemish areas are taught in Dutch and those in French-speaking areas in French. In bilingual Brussels parents must choose the language in which they wish their children to be educated.

There is a further division of the education system, between Church and State. The Church system, which is run by the Catholic Church, is largely financed by the government.

Both systems are strictly controlled to ensure a uniformly high standard of education throughout the whole country. So important does the Belgian government consider education that it spends 25 percent of its budget on education and cultural activities.

Children begin school in early September after the long summer holidays and this is a time of great excitement, particularly for those going to school for the first time. In Brussels, both the Dutch and French language systems mount advertising campaigns during the summer in an attempt to influence parents in their choice of school.

Belgian children must study hard as standards are high and there is competition for places in universities and other institutes of higher learning. Belgium has some of the oldest and most respected universities in Europe. The best known is at the city of Leuven. It dates back to 1425 and is one of the foremost intellectual and research centers of Europe. Some of Europe's greatest thinkers have studied or taught there, among them the philosopher Erasmus, who went there in 1518 and founded three colleges. His impact on the university would have been much greater but the Reformation, the great religious upheaval of the 16th century, interrupted his work. After four years at the university, Erasmus moved to Anderlecht, a suburb of Brussels. The house in which he lived is maintained as a shrine to one of Belgium's greatest residents.

Until this century, all Belgians, whether Flemish or Walloon, had to take their university courses in French. Eventually, Flemish speakers forced the authorities to introduce courses in their own language, but there was considerable resistance to the change. In fact, the university at Leuven split into two; the Flemish-speaking part remained on the traditional campus at Leuven, while the French-speaking part moved to a new, ultra-modern, campus at Louvain-La-Neuve, just south of the Linguistic Frontier.

Brussels has more schools catering exclusively for foreign children than any other European capital. This is because Brussels is the headquarters of the European Community (EC) and the North Atlantic Treaty Organization (NATO). Also, many large international companies have their head offices there. The schools include one which has classes in the language of every member country of

A corner of Erasmus's house, now a museum.

the European Community, as well as several English-language schools and others which teach in Swedish and Japanese.

9

Sports

Soccer is easily the most popular spectator sport in Belgium. Belgium's national soccer league is divided into four divisions each with 16 teams. Each of the nine provinces also has its local league. Best known first division teams on the international scene are Anderlecht and Standard. Belgium's national team has been successful in international competitions, particularly in the 1980s.

Car racing also has a large following and several Belgian drivers have gained international fame. Jacky Ickx was for years a world championship driver. The Francorchamps race track, near Spa, was once considered the most dangerous track in the world of formula one grand prix racing. It was 9 miles (14 kilometers) long with sharp bends which caused many accidents. The track was closed to formula one grand prix events in 1970 but reopened in 1983.

For the more energetic there are excellent facilities for a wide range of activities. Tennis is played all year round, outdoors in summer and indoors, in large covered courts, in winter. Squash is also becoming popular.

The Francorchamps racing circuit.

Walking and hiking are almost a passion for many Belgians who spend hours, often whole weekends, tramping in the forests and open countryside. Hikers are all ages. Family groups, from grand-parents down to small children, hike through the forests, either in the depth of the Ardennes or in the Forêt de Soignes, not far from the heart of Brussels.

Many Belgians cycle for pleasure, especially in the flat areas of Flanders. Many really fit individuals race in competitions.

Horse riding is a costly pastime, indulged in by a wealthy minority and bridle paths crisscross most of the country's forests.

The Ardennes, a hilly area in the southern provinces of Liège and Luxembourg, offer wonderful opportunities for fishing, canoe-

63

A sand yacht which can race along the sandy beaches of the northern coast of Belgium.

ing on fast exciting rivers, hunting, and caving. People go to the Ardennes to hunt a species of wild boar called a sanglier. This is not a domesticated pig that has gone wild but a true wild animal, fierce in appearance and nature, and covered with coarse hair. Several species of deer roam the area and offer sport to the hunter. Rabbits are also regarded as game.

The Ardennes have many deep cave systems which provide an exciting, and sometimes dangerous, challenge to cavers.

On the flat wide, sandy beaches of the north Belgian coast, sand sailing is a popular sport. Sand yachts have conventional sails but lightweight bodies and bicycle-type wheels. They race along the sand at breakneck speed, propelled by the wind.

Skiing is a popular winter sport, and again the Ardennes is the

64

venue. Belgium has no mountains and its highest ski center, at Elsenborn, is only 2,100 feet (650 meters) above sea level. It is one of ten downhill ski slopes and, on winter afternoons when the snow is good, attracts thousands of enthusiasts. Belgium also has 42 centers for langlauf or cross-country skiing, in which skiers cover great distances over flat country or very gentle slopes. The Ardennes are perfect for cross-country skiing and marked trails are up to 9 miles (15 kilometers) long. Belgians admit freely that their downhill ski slopes do not match those of the European Alps, but they have the advantage of being relatively close to the large cities of Brussels and Liège.

Pigeon racing originated in Belgium and sometimes as many as 150,000 birds participate in a major event. Many races start from the Walloon village of Quiévrain—and when races start, the sky is filled with birds.

Buying and selling racing pigeons in the Brussels bird market.

10

Belgium's Cultural Heritage

Belgium has produced many famous painters. People all over the world admire the work of Flemish masters, such as Van Eyck, Rubens, Campin, Van der Weyden, Memling, Hieronymus Bosch, Brouwer, and the Pieter Brueghels (father and son). The heyday of Flemish painting was between the late 14th century and the late 17th century. There are many fine paintings from this period in Belgium, but you can also see the work of the Flemish masters elsewhere in the world. Most major museums and galleries have at least one, despite the fact that they are now enormously expensive.

There was no photography in the days of the Flemish Masters. If you wanted a portrait of yourself, you hired a painter. Some portraits are very unflattering–people are sometimes depicted with little greedy eyes or ugly red noses. These faces are, however, convincing. The painters often managed to reveal the sitter's character in a way which even modern photography cannot do.

Flemish masterpieces hang in museums, cathedrals, churches,

castles and private homes all over Belgium. There are wonderful collections in Brussels, Bruges, Ghent, and Antwerp. These cities were rich and powerful in the Middle Ages. Their upper classes were wealthy and they could afford to pay artists and craftsmen to produce beautiful objects such as paintings, sculptures in wood, stone and metal, magnificent candlesticks, chalices, jewelry, mosaics, pottery, tapestries, and lacework.

To help the visitor who might be overwhelmed by this profusion of works of art, the authorities have selected seven famous works, which they call Belgium's Magnificent Seven:

(1) *The Descent from The Cross* painted by Peter Paul Rubens, hangs in Our Lady's Cathedral in Antwerp.

(2) *The Shrine of Our Lady*, a fine example of the 13th-century art of molding precious metals, is in Tournai.

(3) *The Mystic Lamb*, perhaps the most famous work by Van Eyck, is displayed in the cathedral at Ghent.

(4) Pieter Brueghel's painting, *Landscape with The Fall of Icarus*, is in the Royal Museum of Fine Arts in Brussels.

(5) A small portable cathedral-shaped structure, painted by Hans Memling and called *The Shrine of St Ursula*, is in an ancient hospital converted into a museum at Bruges.

(6) A beautiful baptismal font, 850 years old, by the sculptor Renier de Huy, is in St. Barthélémy's Church at Liège.

(7) The Treasure of Hugo d'Oignies, a collection of early 13th-century portable altars and other church artifacts made of precious metals inlaid with precious stones, can be seen in Namur.

Belgium is also blessed with many architectural works of art.

The Mystic Lamb by Van Eyck, one of the works of art on display in the cathedral at Ghent.

There are gothic churches and cathedrals, traditional Flemish gabled houses and public buildings, and town halls decorated with tracery so delicate that it looks like lace. The town hall in Brussels is a fine example.

Earlier this century, Brussels was at the center of two new artistic styles known as *art nouveau* and *art déco*. These styles influenced many art forms, including glassware, painting, and architecture. Brussels boasts some fine art nouveau buildings.

Belgium has many museums. One of the most fascinating is at Bokrijk, near the city of Hasselt in the Flemish province of

Limburg. It stands on 1,200 acres (490 hectares) of land once owned by nuns from the Abbey of Herkenrode. Examples of historic buildings from all over Belgium are on display. There are town houses, farm houses, barns, windmills, churches, factories, whole villages, and even a brewery where beer is still made. These buildings were removed from their original sites, brick by brick, and reconstructed at Bokrijk.

People in period costume operate ancient machinery and work the farms. An old man in baggy blue trousers, white shirt, red handkerchief around his neck and clogs on his feet, walks through the town of Ulbeck which looks just as it did in 1845. Further on

The beautiful and delicate stonework of the Town Hall in Brussels looks almost like lace.

there is the village of Kempen, which is even older, and by the road there is a milestone which is over 500 years old. The farmhouses are fully furnished, with tables, chairs, beds and working tools typical of their period. There is even a pillory in which criminals were held, so that passers-by could throw stones and rotten vegetables at them.

The Children's Museum, in an old house near the center of Brussels, is very unusual—children are encouraged to touch the objects on display. They can climb into old cars, work cameras, operate machinery and gadgets. They can even make flour by pounding wheat between two stones as the ancient Egyptians did. A particularly exciting feature of the museum is the cave inhabited by dinosaurs.

Music, opera, and dance are important in Belgian life. The opera house, The Théâtre Royal de la Monnaie, is a magnificent building in the heart of old Brussels where the great opera singers of the world regularly perform.

The Belgians love music and there are orchestral and chamber music concerts daily. The Queen Elisabeth Musical Competition attracts entrants from all over the world. The competition, which is an annual event, is held in Brussels and all winners are assured a promising start to their careers as performers.

Dance is popular and Brussels is the home of a modern dance company, officially called *The Twentieth Century Ballet* but known to everybody as *The Béjart Ballet*, after its founder, Maurice Bejart. Classical ballet also attracts audiences and both Flanders and Wallonia have ballet companies.

There are theaters in all Belgian towns and cities, but drama is not confined to the theaters; you can often see live performances on the street.

Puppet shows are very popular. The Toone Theater in Brussels has been staging puppet shows for centuries. Puppet enthusiasts come from all over the world to admire the skill of the master puppeteer, even though they have difficulty in understanding the Brussels slang in which the puppet characters traditionally speak.

Belgium has another, slightly unusual, art form—the comic strip. Belgians have taken this form of entertainment and raised it to a high artistic level. The standard of illustration in Belgian comic books is usually very high. Scenes, people, and events are portrayed with great accuracy, and as comic books sometimes deal with serious subjects it is not uncommon to see adults reading them.

Puppets from the Toone Theatre in Brussels.

The most famous Belgian comic strip character is Tintin, a fair-haired boy created by Georges Remi, better known as Hergé, who died in 1983. Hergé created 23 Tintin books which have been translated into 32 languages, even Chinese. An estimated 80 million copies have been sold. Hergé began telling the story of Tintin and his dog Milou in 1929 and produced the last book in 1976. Other characters in the books are almost as famous as Tintin—Captain Haddock, for example, who has 325 different ways of swearing. Many Belgian and other continental comic books are based on the style and format created by Hergé, who was a highly respected national figure when he died.

The Smurfs—or *Schtroumpfs* as they are called in French—were created in Belgium. These lovable cartoon characters have appeared in television series throughout the world, and have also been made into plastic toys.

The Belgians, like the French, are gastronomes—they take eating and drinking very seriously. Gastronomic skill is highly regarded and people who have diplomas from the country's leading schools of cuisine, or gastronomic clubs or associations, are nationally respected. Belgium's restaurants serve many specialities and people who love fine food travel from adjoining countries just for a single meal.

Belgian specialties include *Waterzooi*—chicken or fish cooked in a rich soup; *Paling In T' Groen*—eels cooked with green herbs; and beef braised in beer. Some classic dishes are made with rather unusual ingredients. *Jette d'Houblon* is made from the green shoots

With food displays like this in their shop windows it is hardly surprising that the Belgians are gastronomes.

of the hop vine, the flowers of which are used in brewing beer. This dish is available only for a limited period while the hop vine is at a certain stage. Another classic dish, made from the shoots of the asparagus plant, is called *Asparagus à la Flamande*—which means in the Flemish style. The asparagus is served with melted butter, chopped parsley and hard-boiled eggs. Yet another favorite Belgian vegetable is witloof or chicory, which is eaten raw in a salad, or baked in white sauce. While discussing vegetables we must not forget the Brussels sprout, which has been grown in Belgian kitchen gardens for hundreds of years. They are suited to the climate as they thrive in cold weather and are one of the few locally-grown vegetables available in mid-winter.

73

This boy is eating a favorite Belgian food—chips served in a cone of paper and topped with mayonnaise.

Although the cuisine is first rate, many Belgians still love simple foods, and one favorite is potato chips (french fries), which the Belgians call *frites*. There are chip stalls dotted along most major highways. A favorite dish, served in even the best restaurants, is mussels and chips. This may sound an odd combination, but mussels steamed in wine and their own juice are perfect partners to crisp potatoes.

11

Land of Festivals

All Belgians love festivals. Carnivals and parades are held through-out the year but March (before Lent) is the most popular month for these festivities. On a Sunday in mid-March there may be parades in as many as 20 towns.

One of the best known of Belgium's festivals is *Ommegang*. This is held on the first Thursday in July, in the Great Market, a square in the center of Brussels. Ommegang means "walk around." We do not know when the first Ommegang was held but there are records dating back to 1359. It is religious in origin—the priests of Brussels used to process around the walled city carrying a small wooden statue of the Virgin Mary, which is usually kept in a church called Our Lady of the Sablon. Gradually, however, the Ommegang became more secular. The 1549 Ommegang was recorded in great detail and the modern festival adheres closely to that description. Each year, more than 2,200 people in brilliantly colored costumes take part in the procession. There are mythical creatures, real ani-mals and over 300 flags.

A scene during the Brussels Ommegang when more than 2,000 people take part in the procession.

The Ommegang was not held between 1580 and 1930, except for one special performance put on for the Emperor Napoleon and his wife, Maria Louisa. The Ommegang was revived in 1930 to commemorate the 550th anniversary of the Royal Guild of Crossbowmen of St. George. It has been held annually since, except during World War II.

Perhaps the most famous carnival characters are the Gilles from the medieval Walloon city of Binche. They wear elaborate and beautiful costumes and spectacular headgear four feet (one and a half meters) high, made from ostrich feathers. These costumes, which the Gille must pay for himself, are very expensive and a Gille is not permitted to wear his costume outside the town of Binche.

The carnival and procession take place every Shrove Tuesday,

76

starting at dawn and continuing all day and all night. The Gilles perform a traditional, shuffling dance which makes it appear that their whole body is shimmering. During the procession oranges are scattered among the crowd. The origins of Binche's carnival are not known, but some elements date from the time of the Emperor Charles V. The Gilles' costumes resemble the clothing worn by the high-ranking Aztec Indians who were captured by the soldiers of Charles V, and the oranges thrown are supposed to represent the Aztec gold which Charles' troops brought back from Mexico.

Bruges holds an annual religious festival, known as the Festival of the Holy Blood, to celebrate the presence of a relic of the blood of Christ. A local nobleman, Thierry of Alsace, brought the relic

Gilles in their beautiful costumes and splendid plumes, seen at the carnival of Binche.

back from a Crusade in the 12th century. The relic is kept in an ornate, portable container called a reliquary which is carried through the streets in procession every May. Although religious, the procession has a wider appeal as many citizens of Bruges dress in biblical clothes and enact scenes from the Bible as they walk through the streets. You may see the tribes of Israel driving herds of sheep and goats, knights, crusaders, noblemen and women on magnificent horses, floats, bands—even the local clergy and police join the parade. The festival attracts many visitors from Europe and beyond.

At Ath, in Wallonia, a Parade of the Giants is held each August, to celebrate the wedding of a giant called Goyasse and the deeds of a famous horse called Bayard. Bayard was a magic horse, who could suddenly grow large enough to carry four people. He is so famous in Wallonia that a huge statue of him, with four boys on his back, has been erected beside the Meuse River at Namur. During the festival, a model of Bayard is paraded through the streets as a mark of respect for his brave deeds in the days when the people of the region were fighting the forces of the Emperor Charlemagne. According to legend, Charlemagne's troops eventually captured Bayard and the Emperor ordered that a heavy stone be tied round his neck and he should be thrown over a high cliff into the Meuse River. But the crafty animal freed himself and galloped away—and it is said that his hooves can still be heard as he gallops through the streets.

The Festival of the Cats is held each year at Ypres, or Ieper as the local, Flemish-speaking people call it. According to legend, the city was once overrun by rats, and cats were brought in to control them. In turn, they too became a menace, because even when the rats were gone, the cats there continued to breed. The local people resorted to throwing cats off the tower of the city's famous Cloth Hall to get rid of them. This unhappy event is commemorated at the end of the procession, when crowds gather in the square by the medieval Cloth Hall. Toy cats are thrown from the top of the tower and people scramble to catch them to keep as souvenirs.

There are many other carnivals throughout Belgium. In the German-speaking city of Eupen the annual carnival, called

The giants of Ath.

Rosenmontag (Rose Monday), takes place on the First Sunday after Armistice Day, November 11th. A carnival prince is chosen by secret ballot and he heads the festivities during which, traditionally, paper flowers are thrown into the crowd.

The carnival at Nivelles features "fights" between people who are dressed in medieval costume and balance on stilts. The people of Mons hold a carnival to celebrate the slaying of a dragon called Doudou which, according to the legend, used to terrorize the neighborhood.

Malmédy has a procession with decorated floats, and hundreds of performers wearing strange masks. At Stavelot the mid-Lent parade is led by strange creatures, called *Blancs Moussis*. They are draped in white clothes, wear frightening masks with long red noses and throw confetti over the crowds as they move along. There is even one carnival, at Tilff-sur-Ourthe, where the costumes are based on that humble vegetable, the leek.

One character who is present at most festivals is the giant. Some are as tall as three-story buildings and many are carried on motor vehicles with the figure of the giant built over a wicker framework. They are of all shapes and represent a range of mythical and legendary figures—some are friendly but some are fearsome.

12

Brussels: Capital of Europe

The city of Brussels comprises 19 municipalities with a population of about 990,000. Strictly speaking, the Municipality of Brussels is merely one of these 19 and has 137,738 inhabitants. But when we talk about Brussels, we usually mean the entire metropolitan area and not just a single municipality.

Brussels is not just the capital of Belgium—it is also the capital of Europe because it is the headquarters of the European Community (EC). The Community is a group of ten European nations—Belgium, Luxembourg, the Netherlands, Germany, Italy, Denmark, France, Britain, Ireland and Greece—which have banded together in an attempt to rationalize trade between themselves and with countries outside the Community, and to try to bring about other changes that will be of benefit to all ten countries. The European Community has now become part of the larger European Union.

Belgium was a founding member and Brussels, geographically at the center of the Community, was a logical site for many of its

institutions. More than 10,000 people from all ten member countries work in Brussels at the European Commission. The Commission is the Community's civil service where many laws and proposals are drafted and the day-to-day tasks of running a community, in which 271,000,000 people live, are carried out.

Brussels is also the headquarters of NATO, the North Atlantic Treaty Organization. NATO, of which Belgium is an important member, is a group of countries which have united to defend Western Europe.

Another important defense establishment, SHAPE, has its headquarters just south of Brussels at Mons. SHAPE means Supreme Headquarters Allied Personnel in Europe.

Many multinational companies have their European headquarters in Brussels. They have selected Brussels because it is only three hours by car from Bonn, Paris, or The Hague, and many other important European cities, and it is only three hours by plane from many parts of Africa and the Middle East. Another important factor is that Brussels is not as expensive as many other European cities. And finally, Brussels is a very beautiful city which, though relatively small, is nevertheless a sophisticated international capital.

Unlike many Belgian cities, Brussels did not start as a Roman garrison or a Celtic or Frankish settlement—its origins are much later. In 979 A.D. a nobleman, the Duke of Lower Lotharingia, built a castle on one of three islands which lay close together in the Senne River. People from the area set up stalls, to sell their produce, around the castle walls. It soon became evident that the situation, on the road between Cologne and Bruges, then two relatively big towns, was excellent for trade. Gradually, a settlement sprang up and, only 100 years after the castle was built, Brussels was a thriving town. A city wall, the first of several, was constructed. Another wall enclosing a larger, heart-shaped, area was built 300 years later. This is still the shape of the center of the modern city and the heart has become a symbol of Brussels.

Parts of the Senne River were built over and finally, in 1874, what was left within the city was channeled through a brick drain. The city probably owes its name to this hidden river for it is possible, that the name Brussels—*Bruxelles* in French and *Brussel* in Dutch—comes from the words "*broech*" meaning brook and "*sele*" which means dwelling.

The site where the traders first built their market stalls still exists in the heart of modern Brussels. The Great Market (the *Grote Markt* in Dutch and the *Grand' Place* in French) is without question one of the most beautiful city squares in the world. In medieval times it was surrounded by the magnificent homes of wealthy citizens and the headquarters of merchants' guilds, but an invading French army bombarded the square in 1695, destroying most of the buildings. The industrious citizens rebuilt the square so that it was more splendid than ever and it remains the nation's most popular tourist attraction. Among the intricate, yet stately, buildings which surround it are the Brussels Town Hall and the King's House. The square is paved with cobblestones and in summer the outdoor cafés around it add color and gaiety. Once every five

A carpet of flowers in the Brussels Great Market.

The King's House which fronts on the Great Market in Brussels.

years the entire surface of the square is covered with a carpet of flowers—a breathtaking sight.

The Galleries St. Hubert, near the Great Market, is Europe's oldest, continuously-used, covered shopping arcade. A classic of mid-19th-century architecture, it was built in 1846 and many arcades throughout Europe were modeled on it.

Other relics of the past are the small narrow streets radiating from the Great Market. They contain many restaurants, some in buildings which are centuries old. These streets are thronged with tourists enjoying the wonderful cuisine and charm throughout the year.

Brussels is a maze of crowded, narrow streets and wide boulevards, lined with well-stocked department stores, small shops and bustling markets. There is a large market near the Midi railway station where you can buy everything from clothing to birdseed. A flea market is held each morning in the Place du Jeu de Balle, in the center of a very old quarter called the *Marolles*. Piles of merchandise are laid out on the cobbled surface of the square for the buyers' inspection. The market has the color and flavor of an eastern bazaar, and is surrounded by stalls selling traditional stewed cockles, mussels and many types of sausages. Mingling with the buyers and sellers are musicians who play for coins which the people throw into their hats, or instrument cases, at their feet. It is an excellent place to buy antiques cheaply, but the buyer should be careful that they are "antiques"! For guaranteed, genuine antiques of high quality one should go to the antique market held in the Place de Grand Sablon. This market attracts the experts, many from overseas.

The traditional Brussels house is a narrow-fronted brick building, two, three, or even four stories high. Most have gabled roofs and are hundreds of years old. The Brussels civic authorities are anxious that these houses should be preserved as they add to the charm of the old city—many of them have already been renovated, and modernized inside.

Many people live in suburbs some distance from the center of Brussels. The area near the battlefield of Waterloo is an example of a modern suburb very like those outside American cities. There are some beautifully wooded areas on the outskirts of Brussels where large homes with extensive gardens reflect the high standard of living of their owners. Some people, who work in Brussels and live in the countryside, have the best of both worlds—a quiet peaceful rural environment in which to live, and a sophisticated international city in which to earn their living and enjoy culture and entertainment.

There are some parks and gardens in the suburbs of Brussels and for people wanting solitude there is a 1,750 acre (4,300 hectare) forest, called the *Forêt de Soignes* in French and the

The flea market in Brussels. It is held each morning in the Place du Jeu de Balle.

Zonienwoud in Dutch, which extends far into the urban area. Deer and other wild creatures roam close to roads and human habitations. People stroll, jog, birdwatch, or simply sit under the shade of the beech, oak, or elm trees. More than 30,000 people visit the forest on fine summer weekends, but it is so large that you can walk for long distances without seeing another person. This forest is carefully managed and each year older trees, particularly beech trees up to 200 years old, are felled and replaced by younger trees. Trees are regularly harvested for their timber. The forest is the remainder of an ancient oak and beech forest which once stretched from Liège in the east of Belgium to the Picardy region of northern France. Julius Caesar mentioned it in one of his reports.

Brussels is officially bilingual but, besides French and Dutch, the languages of the other member countries of the European Community are all heard there. Arabic is also quite common because there are many North Africans living in Brussels. But perhaps the most common foreign language is English. An English-speaking visitor who asks for directions in French or Dutch is frequently answered in English.

It is easy to get lost in Brussels—there are few parallel streets and, in addition to having their names up in Dutch and French, they have the habit of changing their names every few blocks. Despite these difficulties, exploring Brussels is worth the effort.

There are many fine buildings and monuments in Brussels. The huge Law Courts, built on one of the city's highest sites, dominate the skyline. There are several castles, including one, in the suburb of Beersel, which is particularly well-preserved and has a torture chamber. The Royal Palaces, the magnificent St. Michael's Cathedral, and many other churches of architectural and historic interest are all worth a visit.

The most unusual building in Brussels is the Atomium, situated in a park north of the city center. It was built as a symbol of the atomic age, at the time of the Brussels International and Universal Exhibition in 1958. A gigantic molecule of metal, 330 feet (100 meters) high, it consists of nine metal balls connected by tubes. There are scientific displays in each ball and visitors travel between them by escalators, stairs or lifts. One of the best bird's eye views of Brussels is from the restaurant contained in the highest ball.

The Atomium, the most unusual building in Brussels.

Another famous sight is the *Manneken Pis*, a statue, about two feet (half a meter) high, of a small boy performing a very natural function. The people of Brussels have great affection for this tiny statue. Nobody knows its origins but according to legend a little boy was lost in the forest many hundreds of years ago and when he was found he was in the act of urinating. The *Manneken* is unclothed—but on certain occasions he is dressed in special costumes. These range from the uniforms of local football teams to ancient military armor.

Trolleys are another special feature of Brussels. They wind around the narrow streets and each day carry thousands of commuters to and from work. It is one of the few major European capitals to have kept its trolleys. Brussels also has a modern underground train system called the A "Metro" which links much of the city by fast underground trains.

Although it is 94 miles (151 kilometers) from the sea, Brussels remains an important port. A canal connects it to the sea via the Scheldt River and barges as heavy as 5,000 tons carry cargo to many parts of Europe. The canal has been recently improved so that soon barges as heavy as 9,000 tons and sea-going vessels up to 10,000 tons will be able to sail to the port, in the heart of the city.

13

Other Cities

Brussels is the national capital, but many other cities are older and were once larger and more important. Because Belgium's population is so large and its area so small most of its inhabitants live in cities or towns.

The second largest city is Antwerp which has a population of 468,000. According to legend, Antwerp received its name from an evil giant called Druon Antigon. Druon Antigon lived a long time ago beside the Scheldt, the river on which Antwerp stands. He used to stop boats sailing along the river and demand a toll from their skippers. If a skipper refused to pay, Druon Antigon cut off his hand and threw it into the river. The name, Antwerp, comes from the Dutch words *hand werpen* which mean "hand thrown away." The legend of the cruel giant ends happily– according to the story, a boy named Brabo drowned Druon Antigon in the river, and from then on the city prospered.

Antwerp has been important for centuries because it is Belgium's major port. Situated on the Scheldt River, which flows into the North Sea, it has been a commercial and trading center since Roman times. Like other Flemish cities, it reached its zenith in the Middle Ages.

Antwerp has had more ups and downs than most Belgian cities. "We owe the Scheldt to God, and everything else to the Scheldt," say the citizens of Antwerp. The truth of this saying becomes evident when we see how the city fared when denied the use of the river. The Scheldt flows from Antwerp and through the Netherlands before it reaches the sea. The Dutch blocked the river for just over 200 years from 1648 thus preventing sea-going ships sailing to or from Antwerp. This caused a serious decline in the city's commercial and trading importance. But the citizens were not beaten. They developed at least one commercial activity that did not require the river transport—the diamond industry. Antwerp remains a world center of the diamond industry. Diamonds from all over the world, even as far away as Australia, are sent to

Work in the Diamond Bourse in Antwerp. The value and clarity of the stones is assessed under a very powerful magnifying-glass.

The statue of Brabo in the Great Market in Antwerp.

Antwerp to be cut from their original rough shape into the beautiful glittering and sparkling gems we see in rings and other jewelry.

Antwerp has always been a center of cultural activity. It also has many historic buildings, including the largest cathedral in the Low Countries. Started in 1352, it took a 130 years to complete and is a fine example of medieval gothic architecture. Many famous paintings hang there, including some by Rubens who lived in Antwerp for several years.

Like many Belgian cities, Antwerp has preserved its medieval central square, which, because it is a Flemish city, is known locally as the *Grote Markt*.

Liège, a French-speaking city, is built on the Meuse, the other major river flowing through Belgium. Throughout most of its history, Liège was the capital of an independent principality. It was ruled by Prince-Bishops for about 1,000 years until 1794. The Palace of the Prince-Bishops is one of the city's most interesting buildings. Another famous Liège monument is a rather oddly-shaped column in the marketplace called the Perron. The Perron was erected by the people as a symbol of their freedom following conflicts between the Prince-Bishops and their citizens in the Middle Ages.

Coal is mined around Liège and it is the center of the Wallonia steel industry.

Ghent and Bruges were among the most important commercial and political centers of Europe in the Middle Ages. These Flemish cities were once great rivals and even today there is friendly rivalry between them.

Ghent is a major port at the confluence of the Scheldt River and Leie River. Its medieval center remains but modern homes and factories have been built on the outskirts of the city. Ghent is an industrial town but the countryside is picturesque, particularly where the Leie River winds among charming villages or fields of blooming flowers.

Bruges is one of Europe's most beautiful, romantic and best preserved medieval cities. The Reie River runs through the city, which gets its name from the word "bryggia" meaning landing stage. The old center is surrounded by canals and by parts of the city wall. Medieval buildings, with narrow fronts and gabled roofs,

A lacemaker in Bruges, one of Europe's most beautiful cities.

give the visitor the feeling of being back in a past age. Bruges's museums and churches contain wonderful art treasures, and many of the historic buildings are objects of art in themselves. Perhaps the best known is the tower or Belfry. Built in 1208 it is 272.7 feet (83 meters) high and has a slight lean. Visitors who climb to the top get a wonderful view of Bruges and the surrounding countryside. They may also wander through the charming narrow streets, visit the churches and museums, and ride in boats along the canals passing under ancient stone bridges.

Dinant, Ypres, Mons, Namur, Mechelen, and Hasselt are also

A street in Bruges, with the Belfry in the distance.

ancient and beautiful cities. Mineral water is found at the small city of Spa in the Ardennes. The Romans discovered the springs and came to Spa to bathe in, and to drink, the waters. People still flock to Spa to take the waters. The name was adopted by the English and used to describe cities where mineral water is found in England.

Durbuy, in the Ardennes, claims to be the smallest town in the world. Although it has shrunk in size (from its heyday in the Middle Ages) to a few thousand people, it still retains its town charter. It is a delightful little place of stone buildings nestling under a castle.

14

Belgium—The Future

As we have seen, Belgium is a small, but complex country. It is rich but has problems. Some result from the worldwide economic situation, others are homegrown, caused by linguistic and regional differences. The process which Belgians call "regionalization," the separation of Wallonia and Flanders, continues as powers are transferred from central government to the regions.

Many Belgians from both sides of the Linguistic Frontier believe there is no future for either region unless they are linked economically and politically. They say "We must move further apart for a short while so that eventually we may come closer together."

There are extreme views on both sides, but few Belgians advocate the demolition of the Belgian nation. For 2,000 years they have suffered because of the ambitions of individuals and states beyond their borders. They have learned that strength lies in the very differences that appear to keep them apart. This is a difficult concept for those living outside Belgium to grasp. Belgians have learned tolerance and understanding of the views and ambitions of

Sailing on the Yser River at Nieuwpoort. The Belgian landscape always seems calm. But sometimes there are storm clouds overhead. The country's prospects, too, indicate that there are some minor problems to be overcome.

others, while at the same time respecting the integrity of the nation and those living within it.

More than any other free, democratic, liberal nation, Belgium faces a challenge. The history of this brave little country should ensure that its people have the capacity and experience to face and resolve the problems that lie before them.

GLOSSARY

burgomaster	Mayor of a Commune Council
Congo	A republic in west-central Africa
frites	Fried potatoes called french fries in the United States and chips in British countries
gastronome	A person who takes drinking and eating very seriously
indigenous	Native; someone or something living, produced, or growing naturally in a country or climate
langlauf	Cross-country running or racing on skis
Ommegang	A famous festival, begun in 1359, held every year in July in Brussels
sand yachts	A small boat-shaped vehicle with a sail and four bicycle-type wheels. It is used in the sport of sand sailing when they are raced at high speeds across the beach propelled by the wind
Saracens	Muslim warriors who conquered much of the Middle East
waterzooi	A dish in which chicken or fish is cooked in a rich soup

INDEX

100